An American Deception's

Revealing America's Dark Skinned Past

Vol. 2

The Columbian Era

Red SilverFox Thunderbird

REVEALING AMERICA'S DARK SKINNED PAST VOL. 2 *The Columbian Era*

For information contact :
InDEED- Indigenous Education Enrichment and Development
http://indedu.org/reneebio/

Book and Cover design by LN Gibson
ISBN: 978-0-9857375-8-0

Second Edition: May 2018

10 9 8 7 6 5 4 3 2 1

3

Table of Contents

Introduction

THE MISCONCEPTIONS THAT PERMEATE AMERICAN HISTORY, especially United States history, are so numerous and abundant that when people are presented with historical facts that deviate from the customary perceptions, they have a tendency to dismiss the information as another conspiracy theory. The old stories from the 'discovery' of the New World to the colonization of the United States are filled with so many fallacies that the retelling of these over the centuries has turned these fictions into truths. The misrepresentations of previous historical writings have become today's realities of the past, not realizing that history has become, using the words of Napoleon, "a myth that men agree to believe".

One of the most prevalent fallacies in North American history is the story surrounding Christopher Columbus and the people he encountered. It is interesting to note that early twentieth century histories were stating that Christopher Columbus was trying to prove that the world was round. However, late 19th century historical writings on Columbus (not school text books) make no mention of this revelation. They do however tell in great detail of the carnage that took place on the islands during Columbus' reign. They also describe in detail of the hospitableness of the indigenous people, the gentle nature of the indigenous people (until they had to defend themselves), and that the indigenous people were considered Negroes.

Eventually, in the re-telling of this story, as history has a tendency to do, facts were being deleted (the man who changed modern history could not be depicted as a slaver, amongst other things), and most of all, the image of the indigenous people and the words and names used to describe them had to be changed to accommodate European interest and values.

As you read this book, it is with great anticipation that you will discover that there is much to learn about the history of people of color on this land mass of North America. We must realize that it was an intention, before Columbus left Spain to cross the Atlantic Ocean, to subjugate the indigenous people that would be encountered.

We must realize that the people Columbus encountered were used as slaves and that the shipping of some of those captured indigenous people back to Spain was the beginning of the Trans-Atlantic slave trade. We must realize that the Negroid people of the islands were no different in the eyes of the European than the Negroid people of Africa. Both of these cultures to the European were fair objects of rapine, captivity and slavery.

Slaves Make More Profit Than Gold

IT IS WRITTEN IN THE COLUMBUS LOGS that on the first day of his arrival to the New World that the indigenous people of the islands "...came swimming to the boats, bringing parrots, balls of cotton thread, javelins and many other things which they exchanged for articles we gave them, such as glass beads and hawk's bells..."1 It is interesting that Columbus brought along hawk's bells to trade with the Native Americans. Author Leo Weiner in his book *Africans and the Discovery of America* stated, "He carried such bells specifically for the purpose of trading with the Indians, no doubt, because voyagers to Africa had found them acceptable to the

Negroes, who used rattles and bells in their fetish ceremonies".2 This means that Columbus knew before he left Spain he was going to be encountering 'Negroes' or dark skinned people in the New World. But how would he have come upon this information, and who were these voyagers? To get a better understanding of how this transpired, one must examine circumstances that preceded Columbus' initial voyage.

What became known as the Age of Discovery or the Age of Exploration grew out of the Europeans desire for wealth. Many European rulers knew that trade with Asia could make them rich, powerful and wealthy, however the inland route to Asia had been impassable for centuries because of the Muslim and Arab domination of those trade routes. The only alternative was an approach by sea. The Portuguese, because of their proximity to the Atlantic Ocean, were the first Europeans to venture down the coast of Africa in search of this sea route and the first to establish trading posts along the west coast of Africa.

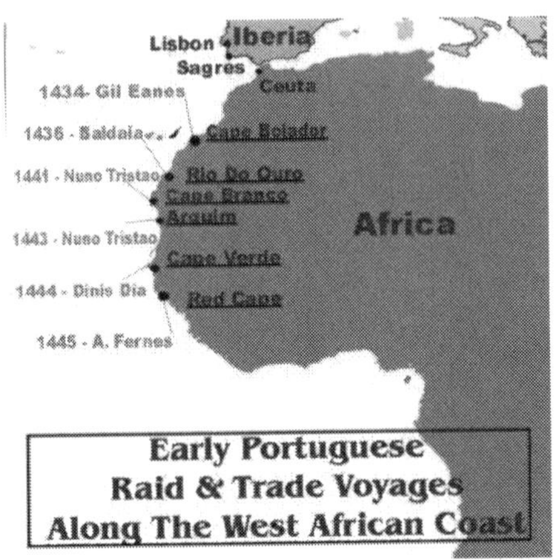

In 1441, the Portuguese for the first time obtained gold dust from traders on the western coast of Africa. The following year, Portuguese explorers returned from Africa with more gold dust and another cargo: ten Africans.3 By 1445, the Portuguese established their first trading post/ slave market/fort in Arguim Bay which in present day is called Mauritania. Up until 1448, only 927 slaves were brought from Mauritania. By 1456, 800-1000 slaves came from that area every year. Eventually, developing royal trade in western Africa took precedence over establishing trade with India.

The Portuguese continued to venture down the western coast of Africa, setting up more trading posts, culminating in 1482 with the establishment of 'Elmina' on the Gold coast of western Africa. The Portuguese, by this time through various treaties, gained exclusive rights to trade along the western African coast, and the building of Elmina was to secure the gold and slaves as a royal monopoly of Portugal. The royal family even demanded that all merchants had to receive a royal license to do business at the Portuguese trading posts. One such person to receive a license was Christopher Columbus.

Present day Elmina(l) and 17th century drawing(r) of Elmina. Built in 1482 to secure Portuguese's gold and

The upper levels of Elmina were for Portuguese aristocrats while the future slaves were kept in dungeons on the lower levels. Pictured on the left is the female dungeon which had steps that led to the

Columbus started sailing at an early age traversing the Mediterranean Sea developing his trading and navigational skills as part of the Mediterranean Trade. While in his twenties he moved to Portugal, after being shipwrecked in 1476 near the town of Lagos. In 1478, he married Felipa Perestrello, the daughter of a Portuguese noble. He was then sailing on missions for the Portuguese government from Lisbon all the way to Elmina. It was around this time that Columbus started to entertain the thought of venturing west to lands across the ocean. It was also this time that Columbus ran into his brother Bartholomew, who not only was working out of Lisbon as a mariner, but also was a cartographer; a creator of maps and charts, and he created many maps of the Atlantic Ocean. There are some historians who say that it was Christopher- with his navigational skills, along with his brother Bartholomew- with his knowledge of the Atlantic, who thought of the plan together to travel to the Indies by a western route.

Even the King of Portugal, Don Juan, knew of these far-away lands which mariners and traders in his African service had spoken.4 Don Juan was even regretful that he did not finance Columbus' expedition, for if he had he believed he would have been the 'emperor of two continents'. Not only was it known that there were lands to the west, it was also known that to the south and southeast, laid another world. The King was certain of this. Africans, he said, had traveled to that world.5 In fact, boats had been found which started out from Guinea [Africa] and navigated to the west with merchandise.6

Two Negroid cultures bartering and trading.

You see, these two cultures, Africans and Native Americans, in the 1400's before Columbus journeyed to the Americas, had a history with each other. The [indigenous] American and African peoples have interacted with each other in a variety of settings and situations. These interactions may well have begun in very ancient times.7 It was this knowledge that Columbus gained from interacting with African mariners and traders that was the pre-cursor of the voyages to the New World. Columbus was not only planning for a western route to the Indies, he knew from his interactions with the African traders, that there was gold in 'those far-away lands'.

One must also presume that while interacting with the African traders, Columbus found out information about the inhabitants of the far-away lands and knew they were of a Negroid stock, which means another possible source of slaves. Even though gold was a very profitable market in the world, slaves made more profit than gold. The Portuguese knew this from experience, and Columbus knew this from his experience with the Portuguese and his personal involvement with the African traders and the African slave trade into the Mediterranean. He had intentions from the start of enslaving the Negro inhabitants from the far-away land

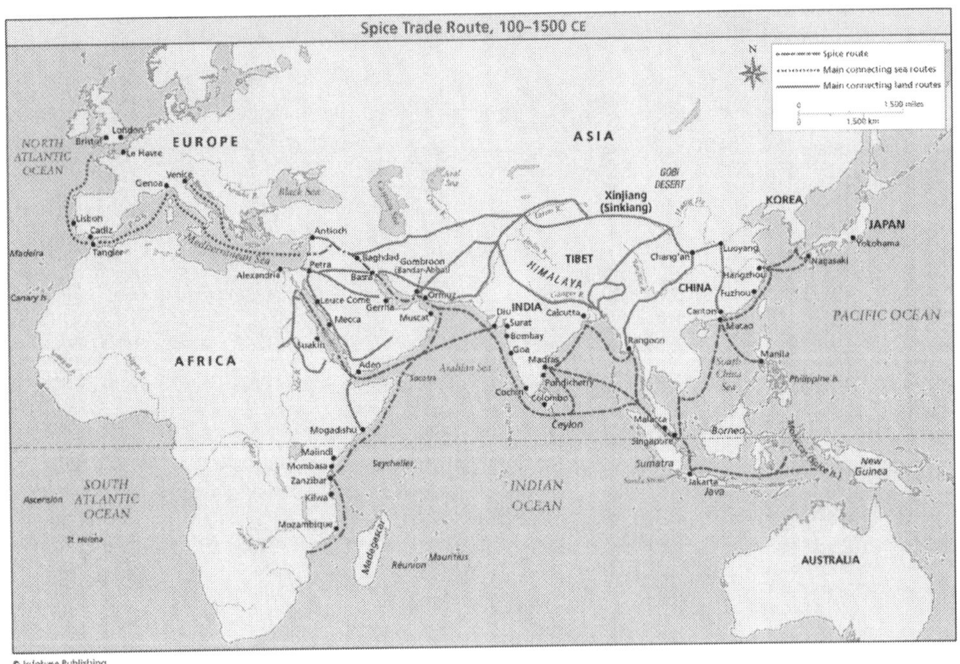

Spice trade routes- 100-1500 CE

Many historians have recorded that the purpose of Columbus' journey was to find another route to the spice markets of China and Japan. The land route had been dominated for centuries by the Arabs and Muslims, and the European countries had been trying for centuries to find a new route to by-pass them.

In the 1480's, Columbus started asking for assistance to finance a new route to the Spice Islands westerly by sea. He first went to the King of Portugal who turned him down repeatedly. At that time, the King's interest was the trade in western Africa, which to him took precedence over establishing any new trade routes to India and Asia. After years of trying to procure funds in Portugal, Columbus left and moved to Spain with his brother.

Columbus' brother Bartholomew and Columbus travelled to other countries to try to obtain the funding, but both returned to Spain with no results. Columbus was in Spain for six years before he finally received a royal proclamation from the King and Queen of Spain. This occurred after Spain finally won their independence from the Moors after the fall of Grenada, which ended eight centuries of Muslim domination of the Iberian Peninsula. Now that Spain was at peace, it could now devote their energies to other ventures and to finance Columbus' journey.

"It Appears to Me, That the People Are Ingenious, and Would Be Good Servants..."

BEFORE EMBARKING ON HIS VOYAGE, Columbus started his log; a daily report of sightings, weather conditions, daily life on the ships, etc. His first entry describes the position of the King and Queen of Spain and how Columbus acquired their graces for this new endeavor:

> *Whereas, Most Christian, High, Excellent, and Powerful Princes, King and Queen of Spain and of the Islands of the Sea, our Sovereigns, this present year 1492, after your Highnesses had terminated the war with the Moors reigning in Europe... Your Highnesses, as Catholic*

Christians, and princes who love and promote the holy Christian faith, and are enemies of the doctrine of Mahomet [Muhammad], and of all idolatry and heresy, determined to send me, Christopher Columbus, to the above-mentioned countries of India, to see the said princes, people, and territories, and to learn their disposition and the proper method of converting them to our holy faith; and furthermore directed that I should not proceed by land to the East, as is customary, but by a Westerly route...8

It is interesting to note that there is no mention of obtaining gold or spices, and if one was just reading this to determine the purpose of the trip you would have to conclude that it was to learn the temperament of the people and then to convert them to Christianity. Consequently, on the day of his arrival to the 'New World' he wrote in his logs, "As I saw that they were very friendly to us, and perceived that they could be much more easily converted to our holy faith by gentle means than by force..."9

Upon his arrival to the New World it was compulsory of Columbus to read a declaration which later became termed the *Requerimiento* or Requirement. The purpose of the Requirement was to absolve all Spaniards of any responsibility for the depravity and horror of their actions wherever they set foot in the New World.10 So, on Oct. 11,

1492 Columbus called his captains and all of his crew "...to bear witness that he before all others took possession (as in fact he did) of that island for the King and Queen his sovereigns, *making all requisite declarations...*"11

One of the many Requirements issued stated, [in part]

In the name of King Ferdinand and Juana, his daughter, Queen of Castile, Leon, etc., Conquerors of barbarian nations, we notify you the best we can that our Lord God eternal Created Heaven and earth...The late pope gave these islands and mainland of the ocean and the contents thereof to the above mentioned King and Queen, as is certified in writing and you may see the documents if you so desire... Therefore, we request that you understand this text...within a reasonable time, and recognize the Church and its highest priest, the Pope, as rulers of the universe, and in their name the King and Queen as rulers of this land, allowing the religious fathers to preach our holy Faith to you...Should you fail to comply or delay maliciously in doing so, we assure you that with the help of God we shall use force against you, declaring war upon you from all sides and with all possible means...we shall enslave your persons, wives and sons, sell you or dispose of you as the King sees fit, we shall seize your possessions and harm you as much as we can as disobedient and resisting vassals. And we declare you guilty of resulting deaths and injuries, exempting Their Highnesses of such guilt and as well as ourselves and the gentlemen who accompany us... 12

After Columbus' initial statement that the people he encountered were friendly, he proceeds to say, "It appears to me, that the peoplc are ingenious, and would be good servants..."13 and three days later states, "...when your Highnesses order it, all can be taken, and carried to Castile or held captives on the island itself, because with 50 men all can be subjugated and made to do everything which is desired."14 It should now be obvious that Columbus' plans were not only to convert the inhabitants to Christianity, but also to enslave them.

During [illegible] not

to incite the native people of the islands offering tokens and gifts, all the meanwhile planning to enslave them and convert them to Christianity. He informed his crew not to barter with the inhabitants so that "when your Highnesses send another expedition to these parts it may meet with a friendly reception". However, immediately after he arrived at the islands, Columbus took a number of the natives by force, and kept them on the ship.15 These natives became basically tour guides for Columbus- directing him around the various islands in his quest to find gold and to determine the disposition of the inhabitants.

On subsequent trips around the islands Columbus detained more of the native people. On one trip five youths "came on board whom I [Columbus] ordered to be detained, in order to have them with me".16 He then "sent ashore to one of the houses and took seven women and three children".17 He says he did this "that the Indians [he already had in his custody] might tolerate their captivity better with their company".18 His detainees however had no clue of what was to come. They probably thought they were 'tour guides' as Columbus stated on one of his latter voyages around the islands that "They were already suspicious because he did not shape a course [back] towards their country".19

As Columbus ventured around the islands observing the inhabitants and their behaviors, he continued to express his thoughts about enslaving them. While he wrote that they were "very gentle", "the best people in the world", "friendly" and "so timid that a thousand would not stand before three of our men",20 he also expressed what his plans were for them on his return trip, writing in his logs several times in various ways, "they are good to be ordered about, to work and sow, and do all that may be necessary, and to build towns, and they should be taught to go about clothed and to adopt our customs".21 Before his departure from the islands he even referred to the Native Americans as "now subjects of the King of Castille"22

Indigenous Americans being presented to King and Queen of Spain.

It is believed that when Columbus returned to Spain

from his first venture he detained approximately twenty five Native Americans. Upon his arrival in Spain, Columbus dressed these Native Americans in their finest indigenous attire, inclusive of many gold trinkets, along with various indigenous plants and animals from the Americas, and paraded and displayed them in order to convey an idea of the importance and the wealth of the newly discovered country.23 It is said that the original intention of Columbus for these detainees to learn the language and customs of Spain and return them back home to the islands. No one knows how many of these Native Americans were aboard the ships on the second voyage; however it is mentioned that two were returned to the islands where one, immediately upon arriving escaped into the interior of the island.

While the accounts of the people of the islands initially were of timid, gentle, friendly people, Columbus' descriptions on his return trip changed dramatically, as if he now needed to have in writing that the people needed him and needed to be civilized. It also appears that from this point forward in history that the indigenous people of the Americas are spoken about in a negative fashion. This seems to begin when Columbus returns to the islands on his second voyage and cannot find the settlement of his crew he left behind.

Toward the end of Columbus' first voyage, one of his

ships- the Santa Maria ran aground and was not able to be fully repaired. Columbus and his crew, along with the inhabitants of Marién (that section of the island) used the salvaged remains of the Santa Maria to build a settlement for the crew members who had to be left behind when Columbus made his return trip to Spain. The indigenous inhabitants under the leadership of their principle chief Guacanagari, not only helped with the building of this settlement which Columbus named La Navidad, they helped to provide provisions, as many of the inhabitants of the islands did for their 'visitors'.

When Columbus returned on his second voyage he found La Navidad in complete ruins. At first it was feared that there had been treachery on the part Guacanagari, in whom the Admiral [Columbus] had reposed confidence and friendship; but the accounts given by the natives tended to dispel this fear, and to convince the Spaniards that the colonists had perished from other causes. Some of them, it was said, had died of sickness; some had fallen in quarrels among themselves; and some, having gone to other parts of the island, had taken Indian wives and adopted the customs of the natives.24 The Spaniards were still not convinced that the native people were not responsible for the destruction of the encampment, however after some exploration they found out that the tribal village of Guacanagari also shared in the disaster that had befallen the settlement.

Indigenous people at La Navidad

While it is recorded that the destruction of the settlement was at the hands of some native inhabitants, what is not readily available is the evidence of the behavior of the Spaniards who were left behind that led to the destruction. Whereas, it is true that some of the Spaniards died of natural causes, and some retreated inland with native wives, what is usually omitted is of the outrageous conduct of the men Columbus left behind.

The men who were recruited from Spain to be the crew for the first voyage were not exactly what would be described as your upstanding citizens. Because of the difficulty Columbus had in recruiting a crew for his initial voyage, the King and Queen of Spain made a proclamation that every person that became a member of Columbus' crew was "to be exempt from all hindrance or incommodity either in their persons or goods" and that they were "privileged from arrest or detention on account of any offence or crime which may have been committed by them..., and during the time they may be on the voyage, and for two months after their return to their homes."25 This enticed all sorts of undesirable personnel to be lured as crew members on this perilous voyage.

The crew, often described as being a refuge for runaway criminals and debtors26 included four men condemned to death, one for murder and three for trying to free him from prison.27 Columbus even later confessed that the men recruited "did not deserve water from God or man".28 These criminals would not only be absolved of all previous crimes they committed, they would be pardoned of any crimes committed in the New World. Columbus' entire crew knew there would be no repercussions of any kind of wrongdoings that they may commit during the entire voyage or any they may commit against the native people.

Pardoning this type of behavior was not out of the norm for explorers, for it was the opinion of the church at that time that "...all babarous and infidel nations who shut their ears to the truths of Christianity, were fair objects of rapine, captivity and slavery."29 Since the Native Americans did not practice Christianity, even though it was known that they were a spiritual people, they were ill-treated and the

Spaniards were basically given permission to, as previously stated, sell or dispose the people, seize the possessions and harm them as being disobedient. Columbus even wrote in his logs that the native people 'believe and know that there is a God in heaven..."30, however this could not save them from the carnage that was soon to befall these unsuspecting people.

While Columbus' first trip was one of discovery and exploration, it appears that the subsequent voyages were for the discovery of gold and the exploitation of the indigenous inhabitants of the islands. Now that Columbus was a Spanish noble and Admiral of the Seas (titles he received from the King and Queen of Spain) he was able to gather 1500 people crowded into seventeen vessels for the second journey. (The first voyage had approximately 90 individuals.) The exaggeration of the gold and riches that could be found in what they believed to be Asia was enough to convince many seeking wealth and fortune to venture across the ocean.

Columbus and his crew

Whereas the first trip's crew was mainly composed of criminals and men seeking to avoid their debts or incarceration, the crew that was recruited for the second voyage was of a higher class of people. These were men who could afford to pay their way, and they were men who were not used to manual labor. They believed they were embarking on an adventure where fortunes could be accumulated without much effort. They were, for the most part, young men of roving and adventurist dispositions with no homes or morals who came on the expedition because it was believed that the Indies were composed entirely of gold. They had no intentions of working or making themselves useful.31 Even though these men came from a higher class in society; their moral values were essentially equivalent to those of the first crew. Gold and riches were the main objective of these new crew members and they would acquire these by any means necessary.

The Tribute

After the arrival of the second voyage and discovering the destruction of La Navidad, Columbus went about finding a new location for his colony so he can continue his quest for gold. Following the establishment of the new settlement called Isabella, the Spaniards went about their mission of finding gold, often leaving the farms they were cultivating unattended because the men knew nothing of farming and they did not accompany this trip to do manual labor. Combine the fact that the colonists could not find the gold in the large quantities that they were expecting, along with the labor that was expected of them, and you have a recipe for turmoil. These outcomes lead to the beginning of an oppressive treatment of the indigenous inhabitants of the islands, a policy that was continued onto the US mainland

and did not end for centuries.

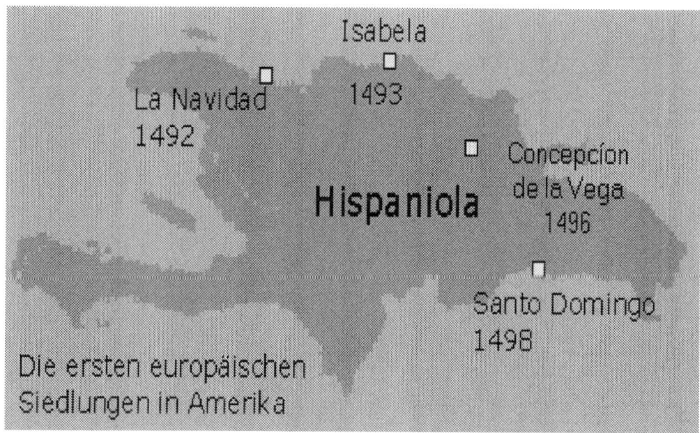

Columbus' main settlements in present day Haiti and the Dominican Republic

One of the first demands of the native people took the form of a system that would augment the Spaniards gold stores and food supplies. Columbus assigned a "tribute" on the native populations of the island where it was expected that "every Indian above fourteen years old who was in the vicinity of the mines was required to pay every three months a little bellyful of gold, and to take for it a brass or tin token, and to wear this about the neck, as a receipt or evidence that payment had been made. All persons not living in the vicinity of the mine were every three months to pay twenty-five pounds of cotton."[32]

Principal Chief of Hispaniola

Guarionex, the principal chief of Maguá (which is the part of the island surrounding Isabella), who up until this time had been faithful to Columbus, tried to convince him to modify his order because he insisted that they did not know how to collect the gold, and the amounts that he was requesting would be impossible for them to collect. (Columbus did not realize that the gold that the native inhabitants had in their possession was nothing more than jewelry that had been crafted and passed down over many generations.) Initially Columbus refused the humble demands of the chief, but he soon realized that the required amount of gold could not be found. As time passed on, it was found that personal service was the only form of tax that could readily be enforced; and, accordingly, more and more of the natives were driven into working the farms [and mines] of the Spanish settlements.[33]

The native inhabitants were not content with the work being forced upon them, and many began to flee to the mountains to avoid their deplorable existence. The native people even tried at an attempt to force their unwanted visitors out of the islands. When they noticed how dependent the Spaniards were on the provisions they produced, they destroyed crops and left the farms in waste, and retreated further inland and to the mountains where they could hide and survive on the roots and herbs there. They voluntarily endured hardships rather than submit to the treatment inflicted on them by the conquerers.[34] The plan was successful for only a short time because the Spaniards still had their resources from home, but also because the islanders had to leave their own farms unattended. It was not long before the native people were suffering themselves.

The plan also angered the Spaniards, who were now advancing into the mountains from town to town to pursue their fleeing workers, and they accomplished this with an unrelenting fury. Villages were burned to ashes. The feeble were mercilessly massacred. Shrieking victims were slashed down by the sabers of the Spaniards. They ripped open the bellies of pregnant women, took out the tiny infants and cut them into pieces. Children were taken by their feet, and their heads were dashed against rocks. Hands were half cut off, and lay dangling by flaps of skin.[35] Ferocious dogs pursued the helpless victims and devoured those that they caught. Others were hung and still others were burned alive. The Spaniards wanted to display their dominance, inspire terror amongst the islanders, and frighten the entire island into submission.

Destruction of village by Spaniards

The natives who did survive these vicious attacks only found themselves in more despair by being corralled on the five ships that had recently returned from Spain, and they were held captive on these ships until they were to depart back to Spain. By the time the journey was ready to depart, sixteen-hundred native inhabitants had been captured. Five hundred of the healthiest between the ages of 12 and 35 were selected to be carried to Spain to be sold there in the slave markets. The rest of the captors were distributed amongst the settlers.

Capture of native islander

This action was the beginning of the Trans-Atlantic slave trade; a policy of utilizing the once entitled gentle and friendly native inhabitants who are now being described as savage, wild and cruel, and using them as a commodity to obtain funds to finance building colonies in the newly discovered lands. Columbus was revising a plan of old to use in the island settlements. It was a plan that was very profitable for him when he was working for the Portuguese along the African coast; to capture the natives, send them to Spain, and to sell them on the slave markets. Columbus estimated that as many slaves could be furnished as the Spanish market would demand, and from this species of traffic a revenue of as much as forty million maravedis [Spanish coin] might be derived.[36] He even devised a plan where the colonists could furnish slaves to the ship captains and receive articles from Spain when the ship returned. The plan had all the cold-hearted brutality of a practiced slave dealer.[37]

No Mercy Was Shown to Age or Sex

AMONG THE PERSONS WHO WERE BEING HELD FOR SHIPMENT to Spain was Caonabo, the principal chief of Maguana. He was accused by chief Guacanagari of the destruction of La Navidad. Caonabo was a very powerful and respected chief and was considered the Spaniards most formidable enemy. He was angry that 'visitors' had invaded the island and built a fort in his dominion without his consent. He was also infuriated that the Spaniards had demanded a tribute from his people, and even more, he was incensed of the cruel and savage behavior of the colonizers and he wanted them off of the island.

Caonabo, along with the other principal chiefs of the island, devised a plan to rid of the Spaniards from Hispaniola. When the Spaniards received word of the plot through Guacanagari (the only chief who refused to be a part of the plot against the Spaniards) they concocted a plan to capture Caonabo. The Spaniards were hell-bent at bringing Chief Caonabo to justice for the destruction at La Navidad. (Guacanagari was the first chief on the island to ally with Columbus and to become compliant to Columbus' demands. When his village was destroyed along with La Navidad, Columbus promised him protection from Caonabo for his loyalty. Caonabo allegedly destroyed the villages because the Spaniards, in Columbus' absence, committed numerous crimes against the native people, and he allegedly destroyed Guacanagari's village in response to

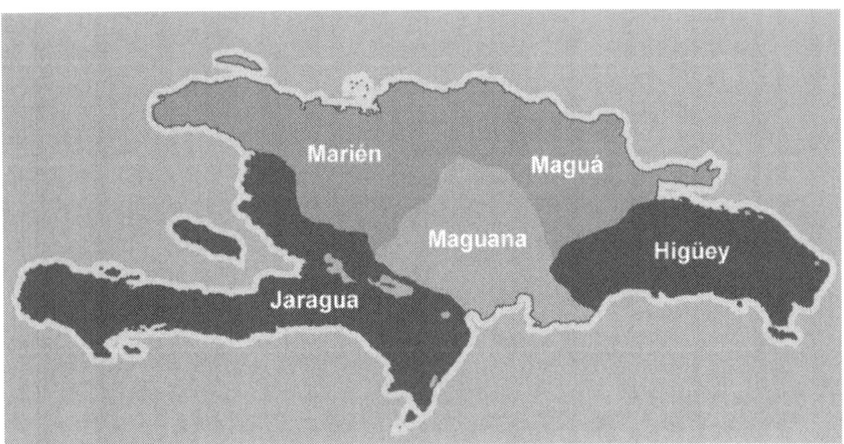

his loyalty to the strangers.)

The Spaniards arranged a fake meeting with Caonabo and his villagers. He was presented with numerous gifts, among them some shiny handcuffs. Caonabo was fascinated with shiny objects, so he was immediately drawn to them. The Spaniards told him he should try them on and Caonabo obliged. Once the handcuffs were secure, the Spaniards took custody of him and carried him back to their ships where he was held captive until the ships sailed back to Spain. He, however, never made it to Spain; he died along the way.

With Caonabo now out of the way, and Guacanagari under Columbus' thumb, Columbus was well on his way of regulating the entire island. Guarionex has now even submitted to the Spaniards, even offering his daughter to Columbus' brother. The chief who now stood the most in his way was Behechio (Bohechio), chief of the most populous area of the island Xaragua (Jaragua), and his sister Anacaona, wife of Caonabo, who appeared to share equal responsibilities as a chief of Xaragua.

Upon Columbus' initial visit to Xaragua, he was able to successfully negotiate a tribute from that section of the island. (Behechio was actually surprised and relieved of Columbus' actions. He believed Columbus was going to capture him, because of his alliance and personal relationship with Caonabo.) Behechio (who later died of natural causes) and Anacaona (who was described as one of the beautiful women on the island, and who took over as the primary chief) remained loyal to Columbus for years. Be that as it may, by the early 1500's, because of the deplorable conditions that the people of the island had to indure, it was believed by the Spaniards that Anacaona and the people of Xaragua were planning to conspire against them.

Under the leadership of Commander Ovando (who was put in charge while Columbus was in Spain), three hundred soldiers armed with guns, swords, and crossbows, and seventy horsemen in full armor with lances, proceeded to Xaragua under the pretense of collecting their tribute. Anacaona, upon hearing that Ovando was on his way, summoned her chiefs and subjects to welcome the Spaniards with the dignity and grace she always exhibited. She entertained them for several days, accommodated them in her best houses, and provided them the best that was available to be bestowed upon them. Still believing that Anacaona was planning a plot against him, Ovando conceived a counter plot which, on his cue, was carried out with a vengeance.

Ovando arranged to entertain the people of Xaragua with the jousting skill of his soldiers. Anacaona and her chiefs were assembled in the house where Ovanda was staying which looked over the square where the show would take place while the rest of the people of Xaragua watched from a short distance. None of the chiefs nor the people of Xaragua were armed, for the entire visit of the Spaniards was received as a friendly visit. Once the horsemen were in place in the square, Ovando gave the cue.

The house where Anacaona and the chiefs were

assembled was immediately surrounded, not allowing anyone to escape. The chiefs were bound and tortured until the Spaniards received a confession from the chiefs that Anacaona was plotting against them. Anacaona was captured and taken away while the house where the chiefs were bound was set on fire and all the chiefs, which is said to have been more than eighty, perished in the flames. The inhabitants of Xaragua were then pursued by the horsemen, trampling them under the hooves of the horses and stabbing them with the lances, swords and spears of the Spaniards. No mercy was shown to age or sex; it was a savage and indiscriminate butchery.[38] Several who escaped from the massacre fled in their canoes...They were pursued and taken, and condemned to slavery.[39] Anacaona was taken in chains to St. Domingo where a mock trial was given and she was found guilty by the testimonies that were coerced and tortured from her chiefs. She was then hung in front of her survivors.

Her memory is still celebrated today five centuries after her hanging. She is remembered not only as a leader of her people, she is known for the ballads, songs, and poetry she created. An 18th century poet Alfred Lord Tennyson even wrote a poem about her, which he never published, giving various unconvincing reasons, but perhaps providing the real reason in an unguarded comment describing "that black b____ Anacaona and her cocoa shadowed coves of niggers---I cannot have her strolling about the land in this way---it is neither good for her reputation nor mine"[40]. Apparently, writing a positive poem about a Black person in the 1800's was taboo, but even more than that, it would reveal that the people of the islands were of a Negroid stock.

By the early 1500's, the entire island was paying tribute

Spaniards pursuing the inhabitants of the islands

to the Spaniards, and four of the five primary chiefs of the island were no longer alive. The last living chief, Cotabanama (Cotubanama) of Higuey, was the only thing that stood in the way of total domination of the island. Despite the fact that Cotabanama was compliant with the tribute, constructed a peace treaty, allowed the Spaniards to construct a facility in his dominion, even exchanged names with one of the Spaniards showing his propensity toward peace, the destructive behavior toward the people of the island continued.

The inhabitants of Higuey (and the entire island) over the years had become very cautious and distrustful of the Spaniards behavior and presence on the island. When the now unwelcome visitors had unjustifiably released a dog on an unsuspecting chief, resulting in the most brutal of deaths, the people retaliated, by killing eight Spaniards. This action caused a war to be ensued by the Spaniards which sent the native inhabitants scattering into the mountains for refuge. The women and children that were found in their hiding places, were indiscriminately slaughtered. Six or seven hundred [people] were imprisoned in a dwelling, and all were put to the sword. Those of the inhabitants who were spared were carried off as slaves.[41] Realizing the prowess of the Spaniards, and their inability to protect themselves against the weapons of the Spaniards, a treaty was ensued which was to protect the local people, on the condition of them cultivating a large tract of land and paying a great quantity of bread in tribute.

When this treaty was broken by the Spaniards, another war supervened. Again, many natives fled to the mountains for refuge and again, they were pursued relentlessly. When they were found, the Spanish spared neither age nor sex; even pregnant women, and mothers with infants in their arms, fell beneath their merciless swords.[42] They wanted to instigate fear and terror throughout the island. The Spaniards were now in active pursuit of Cotabanama and his chiefs; they even took prisoner one of his distinguished elderly female chiefs, who was eventually hanged.

Cotabanama fled to the small island of Saona, off the southeastern coast of Higuey with his wife and children, hiding in the recesses of the mountains. After a long pursuit, he was eventually captured; his wife and children escaping from their hideout when hearing the news of Cotabanama. It was then ordered for him to be publicly hanged, which was obliged. His death was followed by the complete subjugation of his people, and sealed the last struggle of the natives against their oppressors. The island was almost unpeopled of its original inhabitants, and meek and mournful submission and mute despair settled upon the scanty remnant that survived.[43]

They Seem to Show Up in the Slave Markets as Negroes

OVER THE COURSE OF COLUMBUS' FOUR JOURNEYS to the newly found territory, a once populous island that was rich with natural beauty and resources was now virtually depopulated. Some managed to escape by boats to the surrounding islands, and I'm sure because of its close proximity, to the mainland United States. Those inhabitants who remained were doomed to a life of deplorable slavery where there was no escape or hope for the future.

By the early 1500's, the demographics of the islands was

changing, and the need for slaves was increasing. In part, because of the depopulation of Hispaniola, but also because the Europeans were venturing to other parts of the Americas and setting up settlements. The workers for these settlements became the indigenous people, and over time slave raiding (kidnapping) became the standard to obtain these workers. After 1510, Spanish slave raiding reached out increasingly towards the outer islands of the Caribbean and the adjacent mainlands. Much of the raiding was designed to meet the labor needs of Haiti (where the native population was being greatly reduced), but numerous Spanish expeditions captured [Native] Americans who were taken to Spain. By the 1520s slave-raiding in Florida and the Carolina coast area was common also.[44]

Dark skinned people of the Americas

In any case, between the years 1492 and 1501, at least 3,000 Native Americans were known to be shipped to Europe, with the likely total being possibly double that. Most were sent to the Seville area, where they seem to show up in the slave markets as negros.[45] What most people don't realize is Negro was a terminology that was used to describe the indigenous people of the Americas.

Up until the 17th century, terminologies that were used to describe people were of a non-racial origin because ones appearance, as a means of identification and specification, was more significant than that of racial ideology. Anyone with a dark complexion, regardless of their country of origin, was called Negro and along with the misnomer Indian, Negro was also used to define the indigenous people. We make a huge mistake when we apply 21st century sensibilities to terminologies that were created in the past. There were many terms in many different languages that were utilized to define the people of color here in the United States, and many times these terms meanings changed over time.

Some terms, like pardo, loro, preto, and moreno, just to mention a few, were all terms used to define people of a dark complexion that have since become obsolete. Even the terminology brown, as used to define people, is not used in the same manner it was used in the 1600's. In actual practice, English 'brown' was originally a very dark color.[46] Mulatto is another terminology which started out meaning the mixture of Native Americans and Africans which eventually became to mean the mixture of Whites and Blacks.

It is interesting to note here that the English terminology 'black' became to be used in an all-encompassing way to describe all the shades of people of color. What is also fascinating is how it has been concealed that the indigenous people of the Americas: were once considered to be Negroes; that they were the first slaves utilized in the Americas; and their transportation to Spain began what was originally termed the African Slave Trade, but has since been properly named the Trans-Atlantic Slave Trade.

EPILOGUE

IT IS IMPERATIVE TO COMPREHEND that up until recent times, the history of the United States and America has been related to the public through European eyes, European standards and a European point of view. And as we reread these stories, we must use caution, as these stories depict the changing attitude of a people of a darker complexion, and not necessarily an accurate depiction of actual events. We must comprehend that the changing attitude was as a result of the greed of the Europeans and their desire for wealth and to gain and control the newly discovered lands, and their need of a servile population that would help to accomplish those goals.

It is equally imperative to comprehend that this servile population, while being categorized as Negro, were not necessarily, and in many cases, did not arrive here on the slave ships from Africa. The ''brown' indigenous people of the Americas were not only the first slaves used here, but were also the first victims of what became the Trans-Atlantic Slave Trade.

Lastly, it is imperative to comprehend that the tens of millions of [Native] Americans who disappeared after 1492 did not all die in the 'holocaust' inflicted in the Americas. Many thousands were sent to Europe and Africa where their descendants still live.[47] But more than that, those that 'disappeared' did not disappear at all, they got absorbed in the slave population, got re-classified as African, and many of the descendants of those people are living today as African Americans.

About the Author

RENEE SANDERS IS THE CO-FOUNDER of InDEED-Indigenous Education Enrichment and Development, an indigenous non-profit organization which focuses on educating people of the forgotten and omitted history of people of color in what is now the United States. She received her formal education at Temple University in Philadelphia, PA where she received her Bachelor's degree in Music Education. She also received her Middle Years certification and Reading Endorsement from the Atlanta Public Schools in Atlanta, GA.

Educating people has been a lifetime passion of Renee, having spent over 30 years as a teacher in Philadelphia and Atlanta where she has taught: general music classes; band classes; instrumental music lessons; reading classes; language arts tutoring classes; and health classes. She has also worked as a long term elementary substitute teacher and was also the principal of a private day school. Prior to starting her teaching career, Renee spent several years working with children as a music coach and as a summer camp counselor.

Drawing on decades of her music teaching experience where she focused on exposing her students to the evolution of music in America, Renee now focuses on educating people of the under exposed history of people of color in the United States before and after the arrival of the Europeans. She, along with her son and co-founder of InDEED Tavis Sanders, have created educational videos that air not only in Philadelphia and New York on cable television but have also been viewed in over 195 countries on their YouTube channel.

Renee is very optimistic that by bringing to light this previously neglected and overlooked information, that people will have a better picture of the past to use to make sense of the present and have the ability to create a better future for all.

http://indedu.org/reneebio

BIBLIOGRAPHY

1. www.franciscan-archive.org/columbus/opera/excerpts
2. Africa and the Discovery of America- Leo Wiener p.26
3. www.pbs.org/wgbh/aia/part1/1narr1.html
4. They Came Before Columbus- Ivan Van Sertima p.8
5. Ibid p.8
6. Ibid p.8
7. Africans and Native Americans- Jack Forbes p.7
8. www.franciscan-archive.org/columbus/opera/excerpts
9. www.franciscan-archive.org/columbus/opera/excerpts
10. Indians in the Americas- William Marder p.3
11. www.franciscan-archive.org/columbus/opera/excerpts
12. Indians in the Americas- William Marder p.3
13. www.franciscan-archive.org/columbus/opera/excerpts
14. www.franciscan-archive.org/columbus/opera/excerpts
15. Christopher Columbus- His life and His Work- Charles Kendall Adams p.102
16. Ibid p.102
17. Ibid p.102
18. Ibid p.102
19. The History of North America- Alfred Brittain p.160
20. Ibid p.160
21. Ibid p.172
22. Ibid p.176
23. Christopher Columbus- His life and His Work- Charles Kendall Adams p.119
24. Ibid p.135
25. Ibid p.75
26. Ibid p.75
27. A Voyage Long and Strange- Tony Horwitz p.54
28. Christopher Columbus- His Life and His Work- Charles Kendall Adams p.161
29. Indian Slavery During Colonial Times- Almon Wheeler Lauber p.48

30. www.franciscan-archive.org/columbus/opera/excerpts
31. The Real America in Romance-The Age of Discovery 1435-1506 Pt. 1- Edwin Markham p.303
32. Christopher Columbus- His Life and His Work- Charles Kendall Adams p.160
33. Ibid p.161
34. Haiti, Her History and Her Detractors- Jacques Nicolas Léger p. 35
35. Christopher Columbus and the European Discovery of America- Robert Hume p. 118
36. Christopher Columbus- His life and His Work- Charles Kendall Adams p.195
37. Ibid p.195
38. The Life and Voyages of Christopher Columbus- Washington Irving p.284
39. Ibid p.285
40. Allegories Of One's Own Mind: Melancholy In Victorian Poetry- David G. Riede p.69
41. The Life and Voyages of Christopher Columbus- Washington Irving p.289
42. Ibid p.292
43. Ibid p.299
44. Africans and Native Americans- Jack Forbes p.32
45. Ibid p.31
46. Ibid p.124
47. Ibid p.25

Made in the USA
Middletown, DE
26 May 2018